Ceci's African Kitchen

Ceci Tchakounte Tadfor

AuthorHouse™
1663 Liberty Drive
Bloomington, IN 47403
www.authorhouse.com
Phone: 1 (800) 839-8640

Published by AuthorHouse 04/11/2019

ISBN: 978-1-5462-7884-9 (sc)
ISBN: 978-1-5462-7885-6 (e)

Library of Congress Control Number: 2019901427

Print information available on the last page.

This book is printed on acid-free paper.

authorHOUSE®

ACKNOWLEDGEMENTS

This project has been in the works for more than eight years and at one time appeared to be a dead end. But it has been the encouragement and support I have continually received from friends and family that has been my lifeline in so many ways. I will be forever grateful.

I must first thank my wonderful daughter, Anne-Marie for seldom objecting to take a back seat one too many times. I was always so busy cooking, teaching, and trying to make a buck or two with my developed culinary skills over the years.

Many thanks to the city of Santa Fe, New Mexico . . . my home away from my native land of Cameroon . . . for opening your hearts and mouths to a new taste and adventure in Cameroonian cookery.

Always in gratitude to Janette Fischer and Dave Bluette for their continued review of the following material; to Asonglefack Nkemleke for continuing to offer recommendations for text changes and for putting the Cameroonian local colors of green, red, and yellow in the final project; and to author Jetta Dya Jones for the final edits.

Thank you, Victoria Scott (Santa Fe) for decades of preparing and sharing with others delicious African cuisine and her love of the African continent . . . its culture, the people, the arts, and geographical marvels.

And a special expression of appreciation to Michelle Chavez for giving me the opportunity to be a part of the Santa Fe Community College culinary experience.

Thanks to Chef Johnny Vee for the opportunity to cook with him and his unwavering support always.

A big thank you to Anne-Marie, Nyanda Tadfor Little, Rhiannon Frazier and Pauly Butts Boruch for their contribution in coming up with the book title.

FOREWORD

Cameroon, with its jagged coastline along the Atlantic Ocean, is often recognized for its varied terrain of mountain chains and rain forest plateaus extending from Mount Cameroon almost to Lake Chad at the northern tip of the country. Bordering Nigeria to the northwest and the Gulf of Guinea to the south, natives and tourists alike enjoy an array of traditional African food dishes in the inland capital city of Yaounde; beach resort towns like Kribi; the largest city/seaport, Douala; and the popular ecotourism site of Limbe where rescued primates are housed in a Wildlife Centre.

Like many other African states, food staples found in Cameroonian dishes came from New World (the Americas) explorers and from the Portuguese who arrived in the country in 1472. They brought with them such foods as cassava (a root vegetable); maize (corn); tomatoes; and hot peppers. Depending on the climate and what was grown locally, food dishes evolved and now vary in cooking techniques and staple ingredients such as plantains, yams, and spicy (hot) sauces; and fruits (especially mangoes) - from region to region.

With a population of almost 25 million (2018), Cameroonians represent approximately 240 tribes and three major ethnic groups: Bantus, Semi-Bantus, and Sudanese. Diplomatic relations between the United States and Cameroon were established in 1960 after the African nation gained independence from partial French rule. *Cameroon is referred to as Africa in miniature because it seems to encompass a bit of every part of Africa: the culture, climate, cuisine, languages, and dialects.* Approximately 33,000 Cameroonian-born people live in the United States with the largest population pockets in the Washington D.C. area.

Foods in Cameroon are regionally based and a plentiful harvest is mostly dependent on climate and geography. A staple indigenous dish is called *fufu* made from starchy ingredients such as yams. Cassava is also used and is sometimes fermented before being cooked. One method is for it to be wrapped in banana leaves and steamed or fried. French influences are also found in dishes such as prunes stewed in tomatoes along with a very hot pepper usually ground into a paste. A national dish is "bitter leaves" stewed with smoke fish and ground peanut paste. Spinach is often substituted for the bitter leaves in the United States, partly because of the bitterness but also because of the availability.

It is common in Cameroon to stew fish and beef (and other available meats such as pork, chicken, or shrimp) together . . . a taste that does not always fit the American palate. Peanut-based dishes such as chicken in peanut sauce tend to be popular among Americans, but many Cameroonians find chicken in the United States to be soft and "mushy" since they are used to older laying hens.

Many of the ingredients for Cameroonian food are unavailable in the United States so individuals traveling to their native home frequently bring ingredients back with them, freezing them to save for special occasions. Some ingredients can be obtained from African and other ethnic groceries as well as health food stores, but substitutions are common. Cameroonian Americans tend to be cosmopolitan in their eating habits. There are a number of restaurants serving Cameroonian food in metropolitan areas with large African populations

In the month long observance and celebration of Ramadan, Cameroonian Muslims fast from dawn to dusk. In most regions, a *fete des mouton festival* is celebrated two months after Ramadan to commemorate Abraham's willingness to sacrifice a sheep from his flock. Christians and non-Christians alike celebrate Christmas bringing to neighborhood and family gatherings their favorite food dishes. Big feasts and elaborate meals are prepared and served for special events such as farewells to those traveling and/or moving abroad; coronations; weddings; and funerals.

As the dialects and geography differ, so do the food dishes that are introduced as one travels from continental country to country . . . and as does the native preparation and cooking techniques. It's not too farfetched to conclude that writing a Cameroonian (African cuisine)

cookbook is definitely not an easy task requiring extensive research and travel. People from different regions of the country eat in a variety of ways. They might use the same base foods such as cocoyams, plantain, cassava, and beans but the planning and ingredients might be totally foreign from one household in the same region to the other.

Long ago, young African girls were trained to be good cooks as it was assumed they could land good husbands and this skill would help them become good wives. And as good cooks and devoted wives they were expected to prepare nutritious meals for their meals for husbands, children, and often extended family and neighbors. Mothers took great pride in knowing their daughter(s) could cook and that as the matriarch, she had done her job well in the manner in which the culture requires. A young girl grew up watching her mother, grandmother, aunt, sister, or some other woman in her life cook. There were no recipes. She learned on the job observing and helping in the kitchen. If she had questions, she asked them as the cooking progressed or later on.

By age ten, most young girls are entrusted with the responsibility of cooking for a family of up to fifteen people at one time . . . immediate and extended family members and sometimes friends and neighbors. Besides cooking, young girls are also expected to take care of their siblings and do other household chores. These duties are usually carried out without complaints or resentment. It's part of our culture. It's simply one of many necessary steps carried out in growing up.

The smell of good food always attracts men around the compound to wherever the aroma is coming from. In the African culture, one doesn't have to be invited to come in and share a meal. Thus, a compound that always lets out an aroma attracts hungry stomachs; usually young, unmarried men curious to find out who the cook is. The tradition still holds that one never limits the amount of food being cooked to the number of people in the household because one never knows who will come by to visit. By the same token, a visitor is never allowed to say 'no' when he or she is offered food.

Today, this antiquated mindset and cultural practice has all changed in most African villages, towns, and cities. More and more young girls are going to school these days to pursue an education just like the young men, so therefore they don't spend a lot of their time at home with their mothers learning how to cook or helping them on family farms.

I grew up in a small but growing town called Buea. It was the original capital of German Kamerun (1884-1918). Then it became the capital of the British Southern Cameroons (1918-1961) and that of West Cameroon. This political transition happened when the British Southern Cameroons voted in 1961 to gain independence by joining the French-speaking Republic of Cameroun in what became the Federal Republic of Cameroon. It has, since 1972, become the capital of the southwest province (now region) of Cameroon. Located about 900 feet on the slopes of West Africa's highest peak, Buea has a very refreshing climate. The beautiful Fako Mountain (also known as Mount Cameroon) overlooks this growing metropolis as volcanic soils from years of eruption provide fertile ground for farming.

My grandmother, Mami Ncha, raised me in this town. Whenever she was not at the farm somewhere on the mountain slopes or selling in the marketplace, she was in the kitchen cooking. I always enjoyed watching her combine ingredients without measuring and was eager to help in any way I could. She would give me the task of getting the spices and ingredients ready for the dish(es) she was going to cook. I was always happy to do the job. Sometimes when my siblings and she returned from the farm or the market, I would have the meal prepared. She was always quite impressed.

By observing and helping Mami Ncha in the kitchen as much as I could, I developed a passion for native culinary delights. I would cook and have friends over or cater their social events upon request. It has been this passion for cooking and the joy of seeing people eating and enjoying the food I have prepared that has pushed me into introducing Cameroonian dishes and foods here in Santa Fe. Most of the people who have tasted my cooking have always encouraged me to open a restaurant, but I don't think I am at a juncture in my life where I want to be involved in a project that big. I had tried that venture in the past on a shoestring budget quite unsuccessfully, I might add. I still continue to cook for events around town and enjoy doing so.

Many recipes found in this culinary collection come from the English-speaking parts of Cameroon. Some dishes might be familiar; some might not. One way or the other, I do hope you will find some new dish . . . a new flavor that is appealing . . . one that will make all your kitchen efforts worthwhile. Now with the introduction of "Ceci's African Kitchen" cookbook, adventurous food connoisseurs can prepare these new dishes in their own kitchens. It is my hope that my food blog (Ceci's African Kitchen) – www.cecisafricankitchen.com and this publication . . . a dream come true . . . will help spread the word about the good tastes of African cuisine as well as many other ethnic food favorites from around the world. Ceci Tadfor

Chopfine!

SNACKS/APPETIZERS

◇◇◇

AKARA BANANA

INGREDIENTS

- 10 fingers of very ripe bananas
- 1 small cassava tuber
- ¾ cup gari
- ¼ tsp. black pepper
- Salt to taste

PREPARATION

- Peel and blend or mash bananas
- Peel, wash, and grate cassava
- Squeeze out excess water from cassava
- Mix banana and cassava in a large bowl
- Add gari, pepper, and salt
- Mix very well
- Scoop/batter with fingers or spoon and make small round balls
- Deep fry a fair amount at a time until golden brown

AKARA BEANS

INGREDIENTS

- 3 cups black eye peas
- 1 large onion
- 1 egg
- 1 habanero pepper
- ½ cup water (about)
- Salt to taste
- Oil for Frying

PREPARATION

- Wash beans and remove all skin by rubbing with hands or on a grater.
- Use water to get rid of the skins
- After all skin has been removed from the beans, soak in water for about an hour or more
- Blend beans and habanero pepper with a little water into a very fine paste
- Pour paste in a mortar and start stirring until paste begins to look fluffy
- Add salt, onions, and egg and keep stirring. The mixture will get fluffier.
- Add water (a little at a time) and keep stirring. Don't stop stirring!
- Heat oil until hot
- Scoop with a spoon and deep fry until golden brown

PAP (CORN CUSTARD)

INGREDIENTS

- 4 tbsp. pap
- 2 ½ cups water
- Some milk (condensed milk recommended)
- Sugar to taste

PREPARATION

- Mix pap with 1 cup water
- Boil remaining water
- Pour pap mixture into boiling water and stir
- Keep stirring until mixture is completely blended and even colored
- Add sugar and milk and mix

- *Serve with akara beans or puff puff*

Plantain Chips

Ingredients

+ 15 green plantains
+ Oil for frying
+ Salt

Preparation

+ Wash and peel plantains
+ Slice into thin (round) shapes
+ Heat oil until hot
+ Fry a fair amount at a time
+ Sprinkle with salt
+ Cool and serve

Cassava Chips

Ingredients

- 4 medium size cassava tubers
- 1 tsp. cayenne pepper
- Oil for Frying
- Salt
- Pepper

Preparation

- Peel and wash cassava tubers
- Slice into thin rectangular shapes
- Rinse and put in a strainer to drain excess water
- Heat oil until hot
- Fry a fair amount at a time
- Sprinkle with salt and pepper

SWEET POTATO CHIPS

INGREDIENTS

- 4 medium size sweet potatoes
- ½ tsp. white pepper
- ½ tsp. black pepper
- Oil for frying
- Salt

PREPARATION

- Peel and wash potatoes
- Slice into long thin shapes
- Rinse and put in a strainer to drain excess water
- Heat oil until hot
- Season potatoes with white pepper, black pepper, and salt
- Fry a fair amount at a time

- *Can be served hot or cold*

Corn Fritters

Ingredients

- 6 ears fresh corn (or 1.16 oz. bag sweet cut frozen corn)
- ¾ cup corn meal
- 1 tbsp. baking powder
- ½ cup chopped celery
- 1 habanero pepper
- 1 small onion
- Salt
- Oil for frying

Preparation

- Pick corn kernel from corn cob
- Blend corn with habanero pepper
- Chop onion
- Mix everything together
- Heat oil until hot
- Scoop/batter with spoon or fingers and fry until golden brown

PLANTAIN FRITTERS

INGREDIENTS

- 6 very ripe plantains
- 2 cups of flour
- 1 tbsp. baking powder
- ¾ cup sugar
- 3 eggs
- 2 tbsp. butter (room temperature)
- ¼ cup milk
- 1 ½ tsp. nutmeg
- Pinch of salt
- Oil for frying

PREPARATION

- Peel and then mash/blend plantains until soft (set aside)
- Beat eggs (set aside)
- In a large bowl, mix blended plantains, flour, and baking powder
- Add the rest of the ingredients
- Mix very well
- Heat oil until hot
- Scoop batter with spoon or fingers and fry until golden brown

FRIED PLANTAINS (DODO)

INGREDIENTS

- 8 ripe plantains
- Oil for frying
- Salt

PREPARATION

- Wash and peel plantains
- Slice plantains into thin diagonal shapes
- Heat oil until hot
- Fry plantains until golden brown
- Sprinkle with salt

FRIED YAMS

INGREDIENTS

- 1 small Calabar yam
- Oil for frying
- About a cup of water
- Salt

PREPARATION

- Peel and wash yam
- Slice yam into thin round slices
- Boil yam with a small amount of salt for about 10 minutes
- Put yam on a strainer to drain excess water
- Heat oil, until hot
- Fry yam until light brown

MEAT PIES

INGREDIENTS FOR PASTRY

- 5 cups of flour
- 1 tbsp. baking powder
- 2 tsp. sugar
- 1 cup butter or margarine
- 16 oz. cold water
- Pinch of salt

PREPARATION

- Sift flour, salt, and baking powder together
- Add butter and water and mix well
- Ensure it is firm
- Take dough out of bowl and put on a pastry board
- Use hands to knead dough until there are no cracks
- Set aside

INGREDIENTS FOR FILLING

- 1 ½ lb. stew beef
- 1 large tomato
- 1 cup chopped celery
- 1 medium onion
- 2 tbsp. fresh ground garlic
- 1 tbsp. fresh ground ginger
- 1 habanero pepper
- 1 tbsp. flour
- 2 tbsp. vegetable oil
- Salt
- 2 eggs

PREPARATION

- Beat eggs and set aside
- Wash stew beef and season with some of the onions, ginger, garlic, and salt
- Cook until tender
- When stew beef is done, put in a strainer to drain broth
- Wash and chop tomatoes
- Chop onions
- Blend habanero pepper
- In a cooking pan, heat oil until hot
- Add onions, garlic, and tomatoes
- Cook until a little brown
- Add the stew beef and cook for about 10 minutes
- Add remaining ingredients plus 2 tablespoons of the beef broth
- Mix well and let cook for about 5 minutes

GENERAL PREPARATION

- Preheat oven to 350 °F
- Divide dough into 3 sections. Work with one section at a time
- On the pastry board, flatten dough using your palms and a rolling pin
- Make sure the pastry board is always lightly floured to keep the dough from sticking on the board
- When dough is flattened to desired thickness, use a biscuit cutter to cut out pastry
- Fill pastry and then brush the edges of pastry with eggs
- Flip pastry over and seal with a crimper or with a fork
- Bake for about 25 minutes or until golden brown

PUFF PUFF

INGREDIENTS

- 4 cups of flour
- 1 3/4 cup very warm water
- 1 cup sugar
- 3 tsp. yeast
- Pinch of salt
- Oil for frying

PREPARATION

- In a large bowl, pour water and add yeast
- Wait for yeast to dissolve and then add sugar and salt
- Mix well
- Add flour and mix until batter is smooth
- Cover and set aside for about 3 hours to rise
- Scoop with fingers and make balls. Deep fry until golden brown

BREAKFAST

◇◇

Breakfast is the most important meal of the day. In traditional Cameroonian families, breakfast can be prepared with any food source. In most cases, it's whatever food is left over from the day before. We do have breakfast meals in Cameroon . . . some traditional; some European or Western alternatives; and some totally made up. Try some of the Cameroonian breakfast recipes presented in this section. Try something new!

CREPE (PANCAKE)

INGREDIENTS

- 2 cups flour
- 6 eggs
- 1/8 cup canola oil
- 2 cup cold water or milk
- ¼ cup of sugar

PREPARATION

- Put all ingredients in a blender
- Mix well
- Heat frying pan and brush with oil
- Pour in about ¼ cup of batter
- Spread batter to cover pan
- Cook until golden brown
- Flip crepe over and cook the other side
- Roll crepe and place on a plate

PANCAKE

INGREDIENTS

- 2 cups flour
- 3 eggs
- ¾ cup sugar
- 1 ¼ cup water or milk
- 1 tsp. baking powder
- Pinch of salt
- Oil for deep frying

PREPARATION

- Mix all ingredients in a large bowl
- Heat oil in frying pan
- Scoop about ½ cup batter and pour in oil
- Several pancakes can be cooked at the same time
- Cook each side until golden brown

Corn Custard (Pap, Akamu)

Ingredients

- 4 tbsp. pap
- 2 cups water
- Sugar to taste
- Milk

Preparation

- Mix pap with some of the water to form a paste
- Boil the rest of the water and leave on the stove under low heat
- Pour paste into water and stir continuously
- Continue stirring until you get the thickness you want
- Add sugar and milk as desired
- Serve with akara beans, puff puff, scones, etc.

Rice Custard

Ingredients

- 1 cup rice flour
- 2 cups water
- Sugar to taste
- Milk

Preparation

- Follow directions for corn custard

Chips and Eggs

Ingredients

- 8 large potatoes
- Oil for frying
- Salt to taste

Ingredients

- 6 eggs
- ¼ cup onion (chopped)
- ¼ cup leeks (chopped)
- 1 small tomato (chopped)
- Oil for frying
- Salt to taste

Preparation

- Peel and wash potatoes
- Slice or cut potatoes to desired shapes
- Fry potatoes

Preparation

- Crack and beat eggs
- Pour some oil in a frying pan
- Pour in eggs cooking for about a minute
- Add onions, leeks, tomatoes, and salt
- Flip over and cook for another minute or two

FRIED YAMS AND EGGS

INGREDIENTS

+ 1 small white yam
+ Salt to taste
+ 1 cup water
+ Oil for frying

PREPARATION

+ Peel and wash yam
+ Boil yams with salt for about 20 minutes
+ Drain out excess water from yam and let cool
+ Slice yams
+ Pour oil in frying pan
+ Fry yams until golden brown

EGGS (SCRAMBLED)

INGREDIENTS

- 6 eggs
- 1 small tomato (chopped)
- 1 small onion (chopped)
- Pepper to taste
- Salt to taste
- 2 tbsp. oil

PREPARATION

- Beat eggs in a large bowl
- Pour oil in frying pan over medium heat

Akara Banana

Chips and omelet

Crepes

Plantain Fritters

Dodo and Soya

Puff puff

PEELING CASSAVA

YAMS

FRYING AKARA BANANA

PLANTAIN CHIPS

BLACK EYED PEAS

PEELED BLACK EYED PEAS

FRYING THE AKARA BEANS

Why the Pig goes around with its Nose on the Ground

A Cameroonian Folk Tale

Mebue, the pig and Nufi, the tortoise were childhood friends. They went to the farm together with their parents. They took their parents' harvest to the market together and they always stopped at Menla's, the village store for some palm wine on their way home from the market. The tortoise even named his first son after his friend the pig. Mebue and Nufi were almost like brothers. They even got their tribal marks together.

Nufi didn't like doing any work but Mebue was always able to get him to work if Mebue was also working. Curious enough, Nufi always looked for a way to get out of work whenever he could.

Mebue was a very hard worker. He spent long hours working on his farm making sure he had enough food saved for the rainy season. He always had more than enough saved and Nufi and his family always came to obtain food from Mebue during the rainy season. Mebue was always happy and willing to share the food with his friend.

Nufi liked having a good time. During the dry season, he spent most of the time drinking rather than going to the farm as others did. And so when the rainy season came around, he was always short on food for his family. Nufi's wife, Yomi needed some plastic shoes for the rainy season but Nufi didn't have enough money to buy them for her. He decided to go to his friend, Mebue, to borrow money for the shoes. Mebue was happy to lend him the money.

Six months went by and Nufi still did not give back the money. In fact, he didn't make any effort to pay Mebue back. Later, Mebue came to ask for his money. As time went on, Nufi did as much as he could to avoid Mebue. One day Yomi was grinding some egusi on a grinding stone and Nufi was sitting and warming himself by the fire. Then he heard Mebue telling a neighbor that he was going to Nufi's to collect his money and he wasn't leaving until he got the money. Nufi told his wife, Yomi to put the grinding stone away quickly and use him as the grinding stone instead. He warned her not to say a word to Mebue when he came to ask for the money.

Mebue walked into Nufi's home and straight into the kitchen where Nufi's wife was.

"Nda nda lo o o (hello!)," he greeted.

"O o o (yes)," Yomi answered.

"Is Nufi home?" Mebue asked.

Yomi did not answer. She was rather whistling as she kept on with her grinding.

Embarrassed at the silence and whistling, Mebue asked, "Is there something wrong with your hearing?" Again, Yomi ignored him and just continued with her grinding.

Mebue became very angry at being ignored and grabbed the grinding stone Yomi was using and threw it outside, straight into the trash heap.

Surprised and pretending to be mad, Yomi lifted her head and started crying.

Nufi slowly turned over in the trash heap and walked into the kitchen as if nothing had happened. Realizing that his wife was in tears, he asked why she was crying. Sobbing and stammering she told him, "Your friend here has thrown out my grinding stone which has been in the family for many, many years."

At that, Nufi turned around and confronted Mebue.

"Why would you do such a terrible thing to my wife?"

Mebue answered, "Because she wouldn't tell me your whereabouts."

Nufi moved closer to Mebue and yelled, "So, what do you want?"

"My money!" Mebue retorted scornfully.

"Is it because of that little money you lent to me that you are torturing my wife, Nufi hissed?"

"Yes!" said Mebue rudely.

"Well, I have your money", Nufi lied, "but to get it back you must find and return my wife's grinding stone first."

"No problem," said Mebue, confident the stone was out there in the trash heap somewhere.

He turned around and headed jauntily straight to the trash heap in the hope of picking up the grinding stone. To his utter surprise and embarrassment, he couldn't find it where he thought it had dropped when he tossed it out. Minutes later, he came back into the kitchen and told Nufi he couldn't find the grinding stone.

"Give me the money and I will come back later to look for the grinding stone," Mebue said almost pleading.

"No grinding stone, no money," Nufi said defiantly.

Mebue went back outside hoping he had missed the grinding stone the first time because of his anger. Confused, embarrassed, and his anger abating, he snorted and dug, and looked everywhere, but there was no grinding stone anywhere around the trash heap. Even as darkness began to creep upon the village, he just kept snorting, and digging, and looking.

Mebue never found the grinding stone. Until this day, he still goes around snorting and digging and looking for the grinding stone in the hope of one day going back to collect his money from Nufi.

Soups

◇◇

In Cameroon cooking, as well as in most other African cuisine preparation, there are commonly two types of soups. Broth soups which are commonly called *pepper soup* and stews which can have a wide variety of thickness and are usually prepared with nuts, seeds, and/or vegetables.

Pepper soups are usually served as a one-meal dish. They are sometime served with plantains, yams, coco yams, potatoes, cassava, or other ingredients of one's choosing. Stews are frequently served with *fufu*, rice, plantains, cassava, potatoes, or some other starch.

Soups are a very important part of Cameroon cooking. They are used with almost every meal. Soups are prepared differently from region to region.

Achu Soup

Ingredients

- ½ lb. dried meat
- ½ lb. kanda (cow hide)
- 1 small dry fish
- 1 cup palm oil
- 2 tbsp. crushed kanwa (lime stone/potash)
- 1 tsp. jowe
- 1 tsp. country onion
- 4 cups water
- 2 habanero peppers
- Salt to taste
- 2 bouillons

Preparation

- Wash dried meat and kanda, cut into desired pieces, season with a little salt, and cook until tender

- Wash dry fish, cut into desired pieces, season with a little salt and then steam. If fish is too dry, cook until tender

- Finely ground country onions and jowe

- Heat water and put all meats, kanwa, and palm oil in a different pot or bowl

- Slowly pour the warm water into the bowl with the kanwa, palm oil, and meats . . . then pour back to bowl which had water

- Do this back and forth a few times. You will see the mixture changing from orange/red to yellow. Continue this process until the mixture is completely yellow

- Crush bouillons and then add habanero peppers, jowe, and country onions

- Continue mixing by slowly pouring the mixture from one bowl to the other

- When everything is completely mixed, you will get a perfect yellow consistency

BITTER LEAVES EGUSI SOUP

INGREDIENTS

- 3 lbs. oxtail
- 2 pieces stock fish
- 2 cups dried bitter leaves (fresh bitter leaves are better if you can find them)
- 2 ½ cups egusi
- 1 large onion
- 3 large fresh tomatoes
- 3 freshly ground habanero peppers
- 2 tbsp. freshly ground garlic
- 2 tbsp. freshly ground ginger
- 1 cup oil
- ½ cup ground crayfish
- 3 cups water
- 2 beef bouillon cubes

PREPARATION

- Wash and cut oxtails to desired sizes. Season and cook until tender
- Wash and season stock fish. Cook until tender
- Soak dry bitter leaves the night before to get them soft and moist
- Drain and squeeze out water when ready to use
- Ground egusi; chop onion; blend fresh tomatoes; add remaining ingredients
- Slowly cook for 10 minutes

Catfish Pepper Soup

Ingredients

+ 1 whole medium size catfish
+ 3 medium tomatoes
+ 1 medium onion
+ 1 tbsp. fresh ground garlic
+ 1 tbsp. fresh ground ginger
+ ¼ cup ground njangsang
+ 1 tsp. ground jowe
+ 1 tsp. ground eseke seke
+ 1 country onion
+ 2 habanero peppers
+ 10 cups water
+ 3 chicken bouillons
+ Salt to taste

Preparation

+ Wash, clean, and cut fish to desired sizes
+ Dice tomatoes
+ Chop onions
+ Grind habanero peppers
+ Roast country onion until black, then grind
+ In large pot, pour water and bring to boil
+ Add tomatoes, onions, and salt
+ Cook for about 20 minutes
+ Add fish, njangsang, garlic, ginger, eseke seke, country onion, and jowe
+ Cook for about 25 minutes
+ Add bouillon and cook for about another 5 minutes

Coconut Black Eyed Pea Soup

Ingredients

- 3 cups black-eyed peas
- 4 cups finely chopped fresh tomatoes
- 3 tbsp. fresh ground ginger
- 3 tbsp. fresh ground garlic
- 2 cups finely chopped celery
- 2 cups finely chopped tomatoes
- 6 cups coconut milk
- 6 -8 cups water
- Salt to taste
- Pepper to taste

Preparation

- Wash black-eyed peas
- Cook with about six cups of water
- Add about a teaspoon of salt
- Cook until peas are tender
- Stir in celery, tomatoes, onions, garlic, and coconut milk
- Reduce heat and cook for about 45 minutes
- Add pepper and ginger
- Simmer for about another 10 minutes

Goat Pepper Soup

Ingredients

- 4 lbs. goat meat
- 1 large onion
- ¼ cup fresh ground ginger
- ¼ cup fresh ground garlic
- 4 fresh habanero peppers
- 1 tbsp. jowe
- 1/8 cup njangsang
- 12 cups water
- Salt to taste
- 4 beef bouillon cubes

Preparation

- Wash and cut meat to desired sizes
- Cut onion into two halves and chop up one half
- Blend the rest of the ingredients using half a cup of water until you achieve a fine consistency
- In a large pot and over medium heat put in goat meat, salt, chopped onions, and water
- Cook for about one hour
- Add blended ingredients and cook on low heat for about 30 minutes more or until meat is tender

OKRA SOUP

INGREDIENTS

- 1 lb. fresh okra
- 2 medium fresh tomatoes
- 1 small dry fish
- 2 tbsp. crayfish (crushed)
- 1 fresh ground habanero pepper
- 3/4 cup water
- 1 bouillon cube
- Salt to taste

PREPARATION

- Cook beef until tender
- Cook stock fish until soft
- Cut, clean, wash, and steam dry fish
- Put chopped okra in a blender with about 1/8 cup of water.
- Press the whip button to mix the water into the okra. (This will help chop the okra a little more and bring out more slime)
- In a large cooking pot over medium heat, pour in water and bring to boil
- Add meat, stock fish, and dry fish
- Cook for about 10 minutes.
- Add okra and remaining ingredients
- Cook for another 5-10 minutes

Serve with fufu

OKRA SOUP WITH EGUSI

INGREDIENTS

- 1 lb. beef with bones
- 1 medium dry fish
- 1 ½ ground egusi
- 5 fresh okras
- 2 medium tomatoes (diced)
- 1 small onion (diced)
- ¼ cup crayfish (crush)
- About a cup fresh chopped spinach
- ¾ cup vegetable oil (can also use palm oil)
- 2 cups water
- Salt and Pepper to taste
- 1 bouillon cube

PREPARATION

- Wash, cut, and season; cook meat until tender
- Wash, cut, and steam fish
- Wash, cut, and chop okra
- Pour oil in a pot adding salt and onions
- Stir and keep stirring as you add tomatoes
- Cook for about 15 minutes
- Add water and bring to boil
- Add fish, beef, and egusi
- Mix well, reduce heat, and let cook for about 25 minutes
- Add okra and crayfish, stir, and cook for 10 minutes
- Add bouillon and spinach, cook for about another 5 minutes

*Serve with fufu, boiled plantains,
boiled yams, or food of choice*

Palm Nut Soup

Ingredients

+ 1 can cream of palm nut
+ 4 cups water
+ 1 large dry fish
+ 2 pieces of stock fish (soak overnight)
+ 2 lb. lean pork (or meat of choice)
+ ½ cup crayfish (crushed)
+ 1 medium onion (chopped)
+ 1 tbsp. fresh ground garlic
+ 1 tbsp. fresh ground ginger
+ 2 fresh ground habanero peppers
+ 1 tsp. ground jowe
+ 1 tsp. ground eseke seke
+ Salt to taste
+ 2 bouillon cubes

Preparation

+ Wash and cut fish to desired sizes
+ Steam stock fish
+ Wash, clean, cut, season, and steam pork
+ Pour palm nut cream and water in a pot and bring to boil
+ Add salt, onions, ginger, garlic, and pepper
+ Stir well. Cook for about 20 minutes
+ Add stock fish, dry fish, jowe, and eseke seke,
+ Stir well. Cook for about 20 minutes
+ Add pork, crayfish, and bouillon cubes
+ Reduce heat and cook for 10 minutes

Serve with kwacoco, boiled cocoyams, boiled cassava, boiled rice, or food of choice

(You can also add vegetables to this soup).

Peanut Soup

Ingredients

- 3 cups roasted groundnuts (you can also use peanut butter)
- 1 whole chicken
- ½ cup oil
- 3 medium fresh tomatoes
- 1 6 oz. can tomato paste
- 2 tbsp. fresh ground ginger
- 2 tbsp. fresh ground garlic
- 4 ½ cups water
- 1 medium onion
- 1 habanero pepper
- 1/8 cup crayfish
- 1 chicken bouillon cube
- Salt to taste

Preparation

- Blend the groundnuts until fine
- Wash, cut, and season chicken and then steam
- Place chicken in the oven until lightly brown all over
- In a cooking pot, pour in oil
- When oil is hot, put in salt and onion
- Cook for about 30 seconds
- Add tomato paste and chopped tomatoes
- Cook until all the liquid is dried up
- Pour water and bring to boil
- Add blended groundnuts and cook for about 20 minutes
- Reduce heat and add chicken, ginger, garlic, pepper, and bouillon cube
- Cook for about 5 minutes
- Add crayfish and cook for about another five minutes

Serve with boiled rice, fufu, miondor, plantains, or food of choice.

PLANTAIN PEPPER SOUP

INGREDIENTS

- 4 green plantains
- 1 large fresh fish (of choice)
- 2 small tomatoes (chopped)
- 1 small onion (chopped)
- 1 tbsp. ground njangsang
- ½ tsp. ground jowe
- 1 tsp. fresh ground garlic
- 6 cups water
- 2 fresh ground habanero peppers
- Salt to taste
- 1 bouillon cube

PREPARATION

- Wash and peel plantains. Cut into small pieces
- Wash and cut fish to the desired sizes.
- Pour water in a large pot adding plantains and salt
- Cook for about 30 minutes
- Add tomatoes, onions, njangsang, jowe, garlic, and habanero peppers
- Cook for about 5 minutes
- Add fish and bouillon
- Reduce heat and cook for about another 10 minutes

Pumpkin Soup

Ingredients

+ Pumpkin
+ 5 cups water
+ 1 small butter nut squash
+ 1 small onion (chopped)
+ 1 small habanero pepper
+ 2 tbsp. finely chopped leeks
+ Salt to taste

Preparation

+ Peel, wash, and cut pumpkin (desired sizes)
+ Pour water in a large pot and bring to boil
+ Add pumpkin, salt, onions, leeks, and habanero peppers
+ Reduce heat and cook for about 40 minutes
+ Add bouillon and cook for about another 10 minutes

Vegetable Pepper Soup

Ingredients

- 6 cups water
- 1 cup chopped carrots
- ½ cup chopped bell peppers
- 1 cup chopped green beans
- 1 cup chopped tomatoes
- ¼ cup chopped onions
- 1 cup chopped cabbage
- 3 medium potatoes (washed and chopped)
- 1 tsp. fresh ground garlic
- 1 tsp. fresh ground ginger
- 1 tsp. ground jowe
- 2 fresh ground habanero peppers
- Salt to taste
- 2 bouillon cubes

Preparation

- Pour water in a large pot, add salt, onions, and potatoes, and bring to boil
- Cook for about 20 minutes
- Add jowe, garlic, ginger, tomatoes, and habanero peppers
- Cook for about 10 minutes
- Add carrots, bell peppers, green beans, cabbage, and bouillon cubes
- Reduce heat and cook for 10 minutes

Yam Pepper Soup

Ingredients

- 1 small yam
- 1 medium size fresh fish (whole)
- 2 medium fresh tomatoes (chopped)
- 1 small onion (chopped)
- 1 tbsp. fresh ground ginger
- 1 tbsp. fresh ground garlic
- 1 bay leaf
- 1 tsp. ground jowe
- 1 tsp. ground country onion
- 6 cups water
- 1 fresh ground habanero pepper
- Salt to taste
- 2 bouillon cubes

Preparation

- Peel, cut, and wash yam
- Clean, cut, and wash fish
- Pour water into a large pot. Add yams, tomatoes, bay leaf, salt, and onions
- Cook for about 20 minutes
- Add, ginger, garlic, jowe, country onions, and habanero peppers
- Cook for about 10 minutes
- Add fish and bouillon cubes. Reduce heat
- Cook for another 20 minutes

HABANERO PEPPERS AND PALM OIL

CREAM OF PALMNUT

PALM NUT SAUCE

BEBEH * NJANGSANG * COUNTRY ONION

SPICES FOR YOUR PEPPER SOUPS

Egusi

Bebeh

Tomato Stew With Chicken

Smoked Fish at a Local Market

Achu Spices

Fufu Served With Achu Soup

Itoe's 'Real Food'

(A Cameroonian Joke)

One day, young Itoe came to visit his family in the city. The first day he gets to eat rice and tomato stew but he just didn't seem happy. "How was the food?" his uncle asked. Itoe replied, "Okay, Uncle."

The next day Itoe had puff puff and beans and later in the day he ate achu. On the third day he had roasted fish with miondor. Later that evening, Itoe packed his stuff and said goodbye to everyone. The uncle was surprised to see him leaving as he had planned to stay for two weeks. The uncle hailed at him as he was leaving. "Itoe, did we do something to upset you?" Itoe turned around and said, "For three days I've been here and haven't eaten real food." The uncle asks, "So what's real food?" And Itoe retorted, "Planti and pepper."

STEWS/SAUCES

Cassava Leaves Stew

Ingredients

- 1 medium dry fish
- 1 lb. stew beef
- 1 ½ cups groundnut paste
- 2 bunches cassava leaves (if bought frozen, you don't need to pound leaves)
- ¼ cup palm oil
- 1 large onion (chopped)
- 2 bouillon cubes
- 1 fresh ground habanero pepper
- 2 cups water
- Salt to taste

Preparation

- Wash, cut, and steam dry fish or cook until tender
- Wash, season, and cook stew beef until tender
- Wash, cut, and pound cassava leaves to break down texture
- Put meat, fish, salt, pepper, and water in a large pot
- Cook for about 20 minutes
- Add onions, cassava leaves, palm oil, and groundnut paste
- Stir well, reduce heat, and cook for about 40 minutes
- Check from time to time, stirring to keep groundnut paste from burning
- Add crayfish and bouillon cubes
- Reduce heat and simmer for another 25 minutes

Serve with boiled rice, fufu, yams, boiled cassava, or food of choice.

Egusi Stew

Ingredients

- 2 lbs. oxtails
- 2 medium dry fish
- 3 cups ground egusi
- 4 fresh tomatoes
- 1 16 oz. can tomato sauce
- 3 tbsp. fresh ground garlic
- 2 tbsp. fresh ground ginger
- 1 large onion (half chopped and half blended)
- ¼ cup leeks (chopped)
- ½ cup vegetable oil
- 3 cups water
- 1 fresh ground habanero pepper
- 2 beef bouillon cubes
- Salt to taste

Preparation

- Wash oxtails and season with a little salt, onion, and leeks. Cook until tender
- In another cooking pan, heat oil until hot
- Add salt and chopped onion. Cook for about thirty seconds
- Add tomato sauce and chopped onion. Reduce heat and cook until all juice is absorbed.
- Pour in water and bring to a boil.
- Add egusi, blended onion, thyme, and pepper
- Cook for about 15 minutes
- Add oxtails, dry fish, ginger, garlic, and leeks
- Cook for five to 10 more minutes.

Serve with boiled plantains, boiled yams, boiled coco yams, rice, miondor, or bobolor

Green Njama Njama

Ingredients

- 6 packs frozen spinach
- 1 large onion
- ¼ cup olive oil
- Salt to taste

Preparation

- Defrost spinach and squeeze out all water
- Chop onions
- Pour oil in a cooking pan over medium heat
- Add onions and salt. Sauté
- Add spinach and bouillon. Mix well
- Cook for about 10 minutes

Ndole

Ingredients

+ 2 lbs. stew beef
+ 1 large dry fish
+ 1 lb. fresh shrimp
+ 2 cups groundnut paste
+ 1 cup fresh bitter leaves
+ 2 packs fresh spinach (washed and chopped)
+ 1 tbsp. fresh ground garlic
+ 2 medium onions
+ ½ cup crayfish (crushed)
+ 1½ cup oil
+ 2 cups water
+ 2 fresh ground habanero peppers
+ Salt to taste
+ 4 bouillon cubes

Preparation

+ Wash, season, and cook beef until tender
+ Wash, cut, and steam fish or cook until tender
+ Wash, clean, and prepare shrimp
+ In a large pot, heat one cup oil
+ Add one of the chopped onions, salt, and garlic
+ Stir well
+ Reduce heat and add groundnut paste
+ Cook for about 45 minutes stirring occasionally to keep the groundnut paste from burning
+ Add water, spinach, and beef
+ Stir well and cook for about 15 minutes
+ Add bitter leaves, spinach, and pepper
+ Stir and add crayfish, shrimp, and bouillon cubes
+ Reduce heat and cook for 15 minutes
+ In a frying pan, pour in the remaining oil
+ Add remaining onions. Lightly sauté and add to stew

Serve with miondor, bobolor, fried plantains, boiled rice, boiled plantains, or food of choice

Njama Njama with Egusi

Ingredients

- 2 lbs. oxtails
- 2 small pieces of stock fish
- 3 bundles of collard greens
- 2 ½ cups ground egusi
- 4 medium tomatoes (chopped)
- 1 medium onion (chopped)
- 2 tbsp. fresh ground garlic
- 2 tbsp. fresh ground ginger
- 2 fresh ground habanero peppers
- 1 cup vegetable oil
- ½ cup crayfish
- ½ cup water
- Salt to taste
- 2 bouillon cubes

Preparation

- Wash, season, and cook oxtails until tender
- Soak stock fish overnight to soften
- Rinse stock fish and steam
- Wash and chop collard greens. Sprinkle salt on vegetables and rub vegetables with both palms until water from the vegetables is coming out
- Pour water in vegetables. Rinse and then squeeze out extra water
- Pour oil in pot, add salt, onions, garlic and tomatoes.
- Stir well
- Add water, egusi, ginger, oxtails, and stock fish
- Reduce heat and mix well
- Cook for about 30 minutes
- Add collard greens, crayfish, and bouillon
- Cook for 15 minutes

Serve with boiled yams, boiled plantains, boiled cassava, miondor, or food of choice

TOMATO STEW

INGREDIENTS

+ 3 lbs. oxtail (or meat of choice)
+ 6 fresh tomatoes
+ 2 cans tomato sauce
+ 3 tbsp. freshly ground garlic
+ 2 tbsp. freshly ground ginger
+ 1 large onion (half-chopped and half-blended)
+ ¼ cup leeks (chopped)
+ 1/2 tsp. thyme
+ ½ cup oil peanut oil
+ 1 1/2 cups water
+ 1 fresh ground habanero pepper
+ Salt to taste

PREPARATION

+ Wash and season oxtails with some of the salt, onions, leeks, and garlic
+ Cook until tender
+ Heat oil adding onions, tomatoes, and garlic. Cook until all the water is cooked down
+ Add water and bring to a boil
+ Add oxtails, blended onion, thyme, ginger, leeks, and pepper. Reduce heat.
+ Cook for 25 minutes

Serve with boiled rice, boiled plantains, fried plantains, boiled yams, boiled coco yams, or other food of choice.

ONE DISH MEALS

◇◇

Coconut Rice

Ingredients

- 3 cups rice
- 1 lb. shrimp (washed and peeled)
- (You can also use beef, pork, chicken, and fish or omit)
- 2-3 coconuts (cracked, shelled, washed, and grated or blended)
- 1 medium onion (chopped)
- 2 tbsp. fresh ground garlic
- 2 tbsp. fresh ground ginger
- 3 medium tomatoes (blended)
- 1 habanero pepper
- 8 cups boiled water
- Salt to taste
- 2 bouillon cubes
- 4 medium carrots (washed, cleaned, and chopped)
- ½ lb. green beans (washed, cleaned, and cut)

Preparation

- Pour water in grated or blended coconut
- Strain coconut and save the milk
- Pour 4 cups of coconut milk in a large pot under medium heat
- Bring to boil and add rice, salt, tomatoes, onions, garlic, ginger, pepper, and bouillon cubes
- Reduce heat and cook until most of the moisture is cooked down
- Add shrimp, mix into rice, and add about another cup of the coconut milk or as needed until rice is done
- Steam chopped carrots and green beans
- Strain and mix with rice

CORN CHAFF

INGREDIENTS

- 2 cups pinto beans
- 2 cups corn
- 1 small dried fish (optional)
- 1 cup palm oil
- 1 large onion (chopped)
- 3 medium tomatoes (chopped)
- 2 fresh ground habanero peppers
- ½ cup cray fish (crushed)
- 4 cups water
- Salt to taste
- 2 bouillon cubes

PREPARATION

- Wash and cook beans until soft
- Wash, cut, and steam fish
- Combine corn, beans, salt, and onions
- Cook for about 35 minutes
- Reduce heat
- Add palm oil, fish, tomatoes, and crayfish
- Stir and cook for another 30 minutes
- Add bouillon cubes. Cook for 10 minutes

Egusi Pudding

Ingredients

- 6 cups egusi (ground)
- 2 large pieces of dry fish (smoked fish)
- 2 large pieces of stock fish (mookanjo)
- ½ lb. beef
- 2 eggs (beaten)
- 2 large habanero peppers (blended)
- ½ crayfish (crushed)
- ¼ tsp. jowe (black pepper or bush pepper)
- 1 cup water or juice from steamed fish
- Salt to taste
- Banana leaves for wrapping

Preparation

- Season fish with salt and chopped onion and steam
- Soak stock fish overnight and cook until tender
- Season with salt and onion. Cook until tender
- In a large bowl mix all ingredients together
- Taste for salt and pepper
- Wash and prepare to desired shape and sizes
- Scoop paste into leaves and wrap
- Steam over medium heat for about an hour

Ekwang

Ingredients

+ 8 large coco yams
+ Coco yam leaves, spinach, or turnip greens
+ 1 large dry fish
+ 1 cup palm oil
+ 1 tsp. ground country onions
+ 1 cup crayfish (crushed)
+ 2 fresh ground habanero peppers
+ 1 large onion (chopped)
+ About 6 cups water
+ Salt to taste
+ 2 bouillon cubes

Preparation

+ Peel, wash, and grate coco yams
+ Wash and cut greens to desired size and length for use
+ Wash, cut, and steam fish
+ Boil the water
+ Line the bottom of a flat bottom pot with some palm oil to keep from burning
+ Wrap about a tablespoon of paste in the leaf at a time and place them in a circle leaving a hole in the middle to prevent burning
+ Place pot over low heat
+ Pour about a cup of water in the center of the pot. Cover and cook for 15 minutes
+ Add another two cups of water. Increase heat
+ Add salt, onions, and fish
+ Cook for about 30 minutes checking the ingredients from time to time. Stir a little from the center (if necessary) and add water if required
+ Add crayfish, country onions, pepper, and oil
+ Reduce heat, mix gently, and let cook for about 25 minutes

Njabu's Njanga Rice

Ingredients

- 4 cups rice
- 2 cups crayfish (crushed)
- 1 medium onion (chopped)
- 6 -8 cups water
- 2 bouillon cubes
- 1 cup palm oil
- Salt and pepper to taste

Preparation

- Heat oil in cooking pan over medium heat
- Add onion and stir until translucent
- Add crayfish and continue stirring until golden brown
- Add about 6 cups water and bring to boil
- Add rice and the rest of the ingredients
- Stir well and cover to cook for about 30 minutes
- Check regularly to make the rice is not burning, and adds water as needed until rice is done

(This recipe is in honor of my friend, Victor Njabu Njomo who lost his battle with cancer in July of 2012. Growing up, njanga rice was regarded as a poor man's jollof rice. This was so because things like tomatoes, meats and other ingredients needed for Jollof rice was not easy to come by . . . thus, njanga rice. Njabu perfected this dish and friends and family alike always looked forward to visiting or hanging out with him to sample this dish. Thank you, Njabu. You will be in our hearts forever.)

Jollof Rice

Ingredients

- 1 lb. stew beef (wash and season with salt and some of the chopped onions)
- Cook until tender and set aside
- 1 7 oz. tomato sauce
- 3 medium fresh tomatoes (chopped)
- 2 tbsp. fresh ground ginger
- 2 tbsp. fresh ground garlic
- 1 medium onion (chopped)
- 1 fresh ground habanero
- ¾ cup vegetable oil
- 3 cups rice
- 7 cups water
- Salt to taste
- Mixed vegetables

Preparation

- Over medium heat in a large cooking pot, pour oil
- When oil is hot, add salt, onions, and garlic
- Stir and add chopped tomatoes and tomato sauce
- Cook until all the juice from the tomatoes is dry
- Add ginger, habanero, and beef
- Cook for about 15 minutes
- Add rice and four cups of water
- Cook and add water as needed until rice is done
- Steam mixed vegetables and mix with rice

PORRIDGE COCO YAMS

INGREDIENTS

+ 6 large red coco yams (use white if you can't find red)
+ 1 small dry fish
+ ¾ cup palm oil
+ 1 small onion (chopped)
+ ½ cup crayfish
+ 1 fresh ground habanero peppers
+ Some fresh washed bitter leaves
+ 4 cups water
+ Salt to taste
+ 2 bouillon cubes

PREPARATION

+ Peel, wash, and cut coco yams
+ Wash and cut fish
+ Put coco yams, water, salt, and fish in pot
+ Cook for 40 minutes
+ Add palm oil, onions, peppers, and crayfish
+ Cook for another 20 minutes
+ Add bitter leaves and bouillon cubes
+ Reduce heat
+ Cook for another 10 minutes

PORRIDGE PLANTAINS

INGREDIENTS

+ 6 plantains
+ 1 small dry fish (optional)
+ 1 smoked turkey leg (optional)
+ 2 medium tomatoes (chopped)
+ 1 tsp. fresh ground garlic
+ 1 medium onion (chopped)
+ 1 tsp. fresh ground ginger
+ 1 fresh ground habanero pepper
+ 4 cups water
+ ¾ cup palm oil
+ ¼ cup crayfish (crushed)
+ Salt to taste
+ 2 bouillon cubes

PREPARATION

+ Peel, wash, and cut plantains
+ Wash and cut fish
+ Put plantains, water, salt, fish, and turkey in a pot
+ Cook for about 30 minutes
+ Add tomatoes, onions, ginger, and garlic
+ Stir and cook for another 20 minutes
+ Add palm oil, pepper, and crayfish
+ Reduce heat and cook for another 20 minutes

PORRIDGE YAMS

INGREDIENTS

- 1 medium yam
- 1 whole medium catfish
- 3 medium tomatoes
- 1/16 oz. can tomato sauce
- 1 tsp. fresh ground ginger
- 1 tsp. fresh ground garlic
- 1 medium onion (chopped)
- 1 tsp. thyme
- 1 bay leaf
- 1 cup peanut oil
- 3 cups water
- Salt to taste
- 1 bouillon cube

PREPARATION

- Cut up yam
- Peel, wash, and cut yam to desired sizes
- Wash, clean, and cut fish to desired sizes
- Pour oil in pot; add salt, onions, and garlic
- Stir well and add tomatoes, peppers, garlic, and ginger
- Cook until water dries. Add yams, water, fish, bay leaf, and thyme
- Cook for about 30 minutes
- Reduce heat. Add bouillon cube and simmer. Cook for 20 more minutes

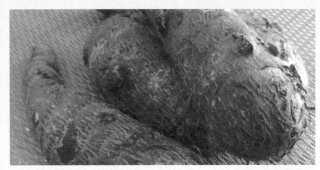

COCOYAMS GRATED

COCOYAMS ROLLED IN LEAVES FOR EKWANG

CORN CHAFF

JOLLOF RICE

EKWANG

Coconut Rice and Grilled Salmon

WHY THE TORTOISE HAS A PUZZLED BACK

(A CAMEROONIAN TALE)

The birds in the forest were invited to a party in a faraway land. They were all very excited about going to the party. Fru, Ako, Bajetat, and Menchub told their friend Nzike, the tortoise who always came to chat and hang out with them about the party. There was going to be a lot to eat, a lot to drink, and great entertainment.

"Am I invited to the party or is it only for you *feathered* creatures?" Nzike asked. The birds answered in chorus. "We can bring guests but we were all warned not to bring you because you always play tricks on others."

"I will be a model guest this time," Nzike replied.

The last time Nzike was at a gathering had been for the naming ceremony of Menchub's first child. The women had spent days preparing the special dishes like *kontri planti, nkui, ndole, njama-njama, goat pepper soup,* and *achu soup* with *fufu.* While all the guests were at the village grove performing the rites for the naming ceremony, Nzike had arranged with his friends to come to Menchub's house and steal all the *achu soup* and *fufu.* When it was discovered after the ceremony that Nzike was the culprit, he was banned from ever attending any gathering in the village of *Nkong.*

Word about Nzike's ban spread all over the surrounding villages. From then on, Nzike had kept a low profile. At the news about an upcoming party, he felt it had been quite some time since his last mischief. He thought time had come to try another trick and add to his shell. On that, he pleaded: "But, that was such a long time ago. I have missed some of the best parties in the neighboring villages since then and I've learned my lesson. Please, take me with you. I'm your friend."

"Ako, what do you think?" asked Bajetat.

"Chui chui chui chui chui …"

"Stop it!" screamed Nzike. "You were asked a question. Why don't you just answer it?"

"There is nothing to think, Bajetat. Nzike can never change. It's like believing that a leopard can get rid of its spots. Trickery is in his DNA."

"Menchub, I still remember what happened at your house several years ago. We were all very disappointed and angry with Nzike," Fru interjected.

"I believe he has learned his lesson. Besides, we've stayed friends with him, and he's never done anything since then for us to now question his sincerity. I think we should take him to the party and stand behind him as his friends," Fru concluded convincingly.

"Thank you, Fru. I promise I will not disappoint you my friends," Nzike murmured.

"*Nkolo* is a long way from *Nkong*. I don't think Nzike will make it that far anyway. He can't fly," Ako remarked.

"Eh … eh … but … but eh, I can fly if you all help me," stuttered Nzike."

"What can we do?" Fru asked.

"You could each lend me a few of your feathers. That will enable me to fly with you, and when we get to Nkong together, it will be a strong way to show your support for me to the people there," Nzike replied.

"Or they'll ban the rest of us for life," Menchub mumbled. It was agreed that the friends would lend Nzike some feathers to enable him fly to Nkong with the group.

It was the end of the market week in *Nkong* and villagers were happy and festive. Chief Pokam was welcoming his fifth wife and introducing her to the village. He had invited several guests from the neighboring villages to share in his and the village's joy. Chief Pokam's compound was bustling with drumming, dancing, singing, and acrobatics as the guests arrived. Among the guests were Fru, Ako, Menchub, Bajetat, and Nzike.

All the music, dancing and festivities came to a stop as soon as Nzike was spotted.

"You all wait here. I will ask to have a word with Chief Pokam," Menchub implored his friends.

Menchub went in to see the chief. About thirty minutes later he walked out into the crowd with Chief Pokam who formally welcomed him and his friends.

"If Menchub can forgive and accept Nzike who tried to ruin his child's naming ceremony," Chief Pokam said, "who am I not to forgive? Welcome to Nkong and enjoy the festivities." After all the dancing, singing, and presentation of gifts to Chief Pokam's new wife Ngassam, it was time to eat the great variety of foods that the women had spent several days preparing. There was kwacoco timbambussa, eru, and fufu, "poullet DG", kontri jamma-jamma, Jollof rice, beans and puff puff, and roasted goat. The list went on and on.

Menchub and his friends were shown to a room with a long table laid out with a wide variety of food. They were to share the table with four other guests from the neighboring village of Welli.

"Look at that *table*," Nzike whispered. "I can't wait to start eating," he continued.

"Do the libation so we can start eating, Fru," Bajetat requested. Fru took a bottle of palm wine (matango) that was sitting on the floor and performed the traditional chore. He poured a few drops of the palm wine by the door and mumbled a few words about the ancestors. Just as Ako was about to get some food, he felt someone grabbing his hand.

"Who's that?" Ako asked angrily.

"Well, well …. Let me introduce myself to my brothers here from Welli," Nzike said. "My name is Nzike and I am the only son of Njo Nvonga. After what happened at the naming ceremony of Menchub's child several years ago, my father decided to have a *Menyi Kah Nsih* (priestess) to come cleanse me."

"Nzike, this is not the time. Can we go ahead and eat and you can tell us another one of your winding tales after we eat. We have been traveling all day and we are hungry," Ako barked. Nzike continued unperturbed. "You see, Ako, this has to do with this food. We cannot start eating before I tell the story."

"Make it quick, then," Bajetat added.

"To make a long story short, Nzike continued, after my cleansing by the Menyi Kah Nsih, I was given a new name."

"What is it?" Fru interjected.

"My new name is *Beenfafa*," Nzike said with a smile on his face. One of the guests from Welli asked what *Beenfafa* meant.

"It means ALL OF YOU," Nzike answered.

"What an interesting name," Ako remarked.

"So before we eat, said Nziki, I will like to call in our host so we can find out exactly who this food is for."

One of Chief Pokam's *Nchindas* (assistants) came to the room and the guests asked who the food on the table was for. The Nchinda responded. "The food is for 'all of you'," and then he left. "Now we can start eating," said Menchub.

"How can we start eating when the food is for ALL OF YOU? It is my food and my name says it all," Nzike boasted.

Fru, Ako, Menchub, Bajetat, and the other guests from Welli were very angry. They tried to reason with Nzike to no avail, so they left the room. Nzike stayed in the room and ate all the food. Overfed and tired, he fell asleep with a smirk on his face.

Festivities continued all night with dancing, drumming, eating, and drinking of *matango*. When morning came, guests were ready to travel back to their villages. Nzike roused himself and realizing that it was morning and time to return, started looking for his friends.

"Hey, Fru, Menchub, wait," Nzike yelled when he saw them. "Are you all ready to leave?"

Menchub answered. "From this day on, you are not our friend, *All of You* or whatever your name is."

They all took off on their flight back home. But just before they were to land, each of Nzike's friends pulled off the feathers they had lent to him. As the feathers were pulled and before Nzike could say anything, he fell flat on his back.

The village heard what had happened at Chief Pokam's party and came to find out how Nzike was taking it. Nzike was still lying there flat on his back, his shell shattered in pieces. Aisha, his wife began sobbing as she approached her husband. She picked up the bits and pieces of Nzike's shell and glued them together. Nzike and Aisha walked home together, shame overwhelming them.

Koki Beans

Ingredients

- 3 cups koki beans (such as black eye peas)
- 2 habanero peppers
- ¼ cup palm oil (melted)
- Salt to taste
- 1 beaten egg (optional)
- Cocoyam leaves (optional)
- Banana leaves for wrapping (or aluminum foil)

Preparation

- Wash and peel beans. Soak in cold water until soft. Pour beans into a large bowl
- Blend beans with peppers. (Add a tablespoon of water or two while grinding the beans to help them move around easily in the blender).
- Pour beans in a large bowl.
- Add salt, palm oil, and egg. Mix well.
- Add 2/3 cup of water and mix very well. (Taste mixture to make sure everything is right for you).
- Use a ladle to scoop mixture. Put mixture in the leaf. Bring edges of the leaves together and tie with a rope
- Place in a large cooking pot and cook for about 45 minutes.

Serve with boiled plantains, boiled cocoyams, boiled yams, boiled cassava, etc.

KOKI CORN

INGREDIENTS

+ 10 fresh corns on a cob
+ 1 cup palm oil (melted)
+ 2 fresh habanero peppers
+ ½ cup crayfish
+ Cocoyam leaves (or spinach)
+ Banana leaves for wrapping (or aluminum foil)
+ Salt to taste
+ 2 bouillon cubes

PREPARATION

+ Pick or cut corn kernel from cob
+ Blend corn with peppers
+ Pour corn in a large bowl and add salt, crayfish, crushed bouillon cubes, and palm oil
+ Mix very well. Add cocoyam leaves and mix
+ Wrap with banana leaves and cook for about an hour
+ Serve hot

KWACOCO BIBLE (ENDELEY BREAD)

INGREDIENTS

- 10 large cocoyams
- 2 large habanero peppers
- ¾ cup crayfish
- 1 cup palm oil
- Cocoyam leaves (optional)
- Banana leaves for wrapping (or aluminum foil paper)
- Salt to taste

PREPARATION

- Peel and wash cocoyams
- Grate cocoyams
- In a large bowl, mix in the rest of the ingredients
- Taste for salt and pepper
- Scoop paste and roll in banana leaves
- Fold both ends of the leaves to seal
- Steam over medium heat for about an hour

Groundnut Pudding (Mbum)

Ingredients

- 5 cups fried groundnuts
- 2 small dry fish
- 1 crayfish
- 2 fresh habanero peppers
- Salt to taste
- Banana leaves for wrapping

Preparations

- Skin groundnuts and finely blend
- Wash and cut dry fish to desired sizes
- Crush crayfish
- Ground pepper
- Mix all ingredients together and mix well
- Scoop balls to desired sizes and wrap in banana leaves
- Steam over medium heat for about one hour

Serve with bobolor, miondor, plantain or other food of choice

Egusi Pudding

A Display of Foods and Spices

Eru

Ndole

Sea Bass

Seasoning Sea Bass

Ready for Wrapping and Steaming

Done

Miondor and Grilled Shrimp

Koki Beans

Cameroon, with its jagged coastline along the Atlantic Ocean, is often recognized for its varied terrain of mountain chains and rain forest plateaus extending from Mount Cameroon almost to Lake Chad at the northern tip of the country. Bordering Nigeria to the northwest and the Gulf of Guinea to the south, natives and tourists alike enjoy an array of traditional African food dishes in the inland capital city of Yaounde; beach resort towns like Kribi; the largest city/seaport, Douala; and the popular ecotourism site of Limbe where rescued primates are housed in a Wildlife Centre.

Like many other African states, food staples found in Cameroonian dishes came from New World (the Americas) explorers and from the Portuguese who arrived in the country in 1472. They brought with them such foods as cassava (a root vegetable); maize (corn); tomatoes; and hot peppers. Depending on the climate and what is grown locally, food dishes evolved and now vary in cooking techniques and staple ingredients such as plantains, yams, and spicy (often very hot sauces); and fruits (especially mangoes) - from region to region.

With a population of almost 25 million (2018), Cameroonians represent 240 tribes and three major ethnic groups: Bantus, Semi-Bantus, and Sudanese. Diplomatic relations between the United States and Cameroon were established in 1960 after the African nation gained independence from partial French rule. *Cameroon is referred to as Africa in miniature because it seems to encompass a bit of every part of Africa: the culture, climate, cuisine, languages, and dialects.* Approximately 33,000 Cameroonian-born people live in the United States with the largest population pockets in the Washington D.C. area.

Foods in Cameroon are regionally based and a plentiful harvest is mostly dependent on climate and geography. A staple indigenous dish is called *fufu* made from starchy ingredients such as yams. Cassava is also used and is sometimes fermented before being cooked. One method is for it to be wrapped in banana leaves and steamed or fried. French influences are also found in dishes such as prunes stewed in tomatoes along with a very hot pepper usually ground into a paste. A national dish is "bitter leaves" stewed with smoke fish and ground peanut paste. Spinach is often substituted for the bitter leaves in the United States, partly because of the bitterness but also because of the availability.

It is common in Cameroon to stew fish and beef (and other available meats such as pork, chicken, or shrimp) together . . . a taste that does not always fit the American palate. Peanut-based dishes such as chicken in peanut sauce tend to be popular among Americans, but many Cameroonians find chicken in the United States to be soft and "mushy" since they are used to older laying hens.

Many of the ingredients for Cameroonian food are unavailable in the United States so individuals traveling back home frequently bring ingredients back with them, freezing them to save for special occasions. Some ingredients can be obtained from African and other ethnic groceries as well as health food stores, but substitutions are common. Cameroonian Americans tend to be cosmopolitan in their eating habits. There are a number of restaurants serving Cameroonian food in metropolitan areas with large African populations.

In the month long observance and celebration of Ramadan, Cameroonian Muslims fast from dawn to dusk. In most regions, a *fete des mouton festival* is celebrated two months after Ramadan to commemorate Abraham's willingness to sacrifice a sheep from his flock. Christians and non-Christians alike celebrate Christmas bringing to neighborhood and family gatherings their favorite food dishes. Big feasts and elaborate meals are prepared and served for special events such as farewells to those traveling and/or moving abroad; coronations; weddings; and funerals.

FOOD AND FRIENDS

WHERE TO SHOP

Cultures United
281 W 6th St
Lowell, MA 01850

African Central Market
63 Fletcher Street
Lowell, MA 01854

Zenith Market
1606 Central Ave SE
Albuquerque, NM 87106

Weyonne International Grocery Store
510 S. Van Dorn Street
Alexandria, VA 22304

Kumasi Supermarket
14790 Build America Dr.
Woodbridge, VA 22191

Tema African and Caribbean Market
17455 Jefferson Davies Hwy
Dumfries, VA 22026

Evergreen Tropical Food Store
2401 Clay Road SW
Austell, GA 30106

Cayce Food Inc.
1680 Roswell St. SE
Smyrna, GA 30080

Makola African Supermarket
1017 - 1019 W Wilson Ave
Chicago, IL 60640

PHOTOGRAPHY CREDITS

Julien McRoberts (Cover Page and more)
Gervase Ndoko
Jen Klafeld
Judith Tadfor
Anne-Marie Nyanda Tadfor Little
Tom Waters
Steven Oliver
Ali
Kamjou Tadfor
Issa Nyaphaga
Jay Alderson III
Will Fischer
Shannon Mokorro
Haddison Etchu
Chika Anomnachi
Ceci Tchakounte Tadfor

GLOSSARY

- Akara Banana – fried banana cake
- Akara Beans – fried bean cake
- Bobolor – fermented cassava ground, wrapped in banana leaves and steamed
- Calabar yam – a large root tuber similar to cassava and potatoes
- Country onion – Cameroon native spice
- Crayfish – dried small shrimps
- Cream of palm nut – cream squeezed from palm fruits
- Egusi – melon seeds
- Eseke seke – Cameroon native spice
- Gari – processed cassava
- Jowe – Cameroon native spice similar to black pepper, with a stronger spicy taste and flavor
- kanda – cow skin
- kanwa – lime stone
- kwacoco – grated cocoyams wrapped in banana leaves and steamed
- Mebue – nice
- Menla – home boy
- Miondor – fermented cassava wrapped in banana leaves and steamed – smaller in size than bobolor
- Njama njama – generic name for vegetable
- Njangsang – Cameroon native spice, oily nuts use for thickening and spicing foods
- Nufi – good things
- Pap – also known as akamu, ogi and eko is a corn fermented custard
- Planti – plantain
- Stock fish – dried cod

Printed in the United States
By Bookmasters